MIX
Paper from responsible sources
FSC® C002795
www.fsc.org

FIRST PUBLISHED IN THE UNITED STATES, GREAT BRITAIN, CANADA, AUSTRALIA, AND NEW ZEALAND IN 2017 BY NORTHSOUTH BOOKS, INC., AN IMPRINT OF NORDSÜD VERLAG AG, CH-8005 ZÜRICH, SWITZERLAND.

THE CHARACTER OF MR. TEABAG IS BASED ON JOHN CLEESE'S CHARACTER IN "THE MINISTRY OF SILLY WALKS" SKETCH FROM MONTY PYTHON'S FLYING CIRCUS.

DISTRIBUTED IN THE UNITED STATES BY NORTHSOUTH BOOKS, INC., NEW YORK 10016.
LIBRARY OF CONGRESS CATALOGING-IN-PUBLICATION DATA IS AVAILABLE.

ISBN: 978-0-7358-4296-0

PRINTED IN LATVIA BY LIVONIA PRINT, RIGA, JULY 2017
1 3 5 7 9 · 10 8 6 4 2

WWW.NORTHSOUTH.COM
WWW.MERVEILLE.BE/DAVID_MERVEILLE/DESSINS.HTML

Monty Python's
Book of SILLY WALKS

By DAVID MERVEILLE

North
South

lways look
n the bright
de of life!
INSURANCE
GROUP
15

Monty Python

10

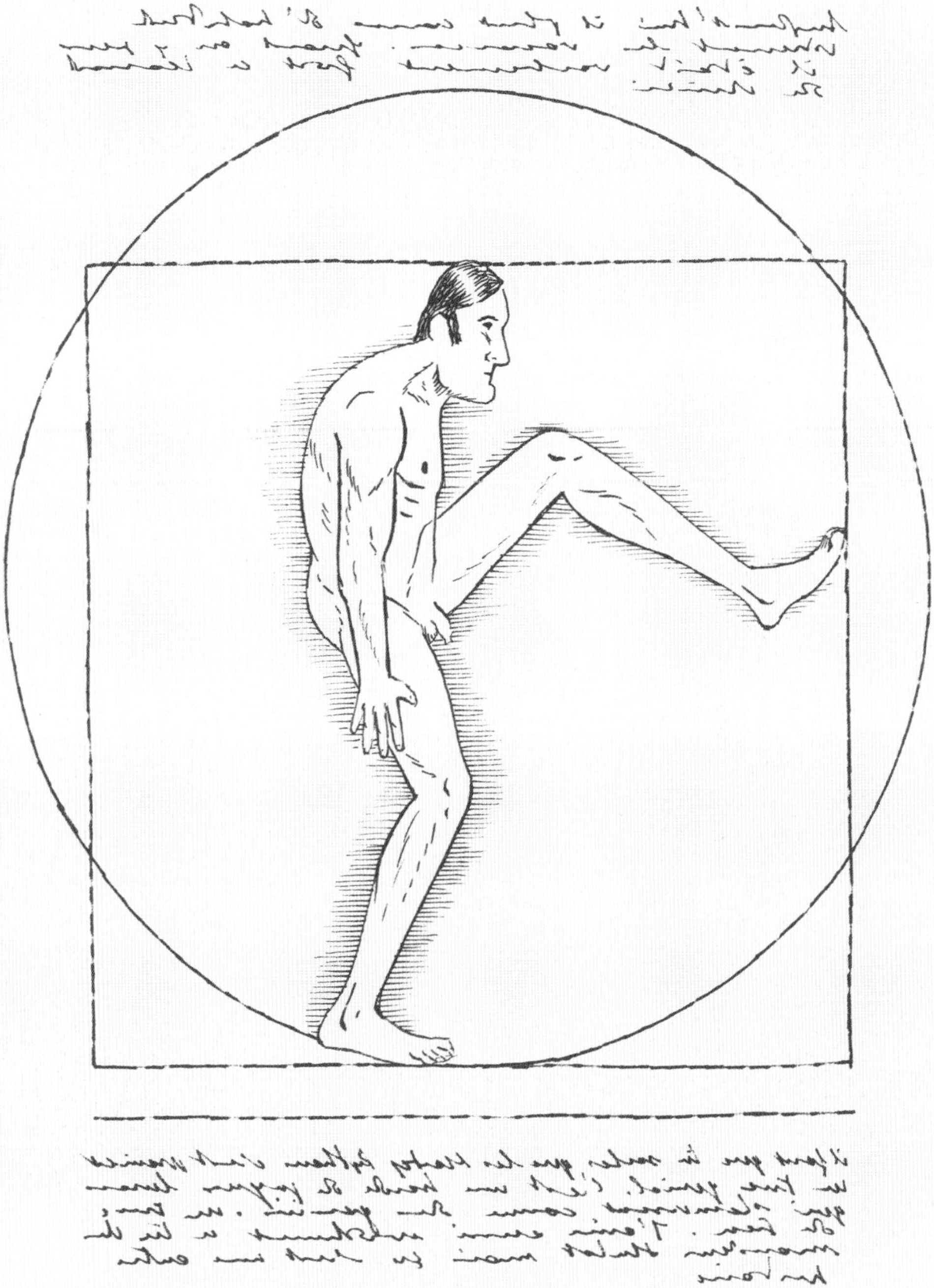

TELEPHONE

91